A Mothering Spirit

K. Lee

Published by Krystal Lee Enterprises (KLE Publishing)
Copyright © 2024 by K. Lee. All rights reserved. Please send comments and questions:
Krystal Lee Enterprises
770-240-0089 Ext. 1
sales@KLEPub.com

To Reach the Author:
Email: me@drkrystallee.com me@authorklee.com
Web: AuthorKLee.com
Social Media All Channels: @AuthorKLee

Printed in the United States of America.
All rights reserved. No part of this book may be reproduced or transmitted in any form or by any means, electronic or mechanical, including photocopying, recording, or any information storage and retrieval system without written permission of the publisher except for brief quotations used in reviews, written specifically for inclusion in a newspaper, blog, magazine, or academic paper.

ISBN: 978-1-945066-67-2

Thank you to every mother who has a heart for children, thank you.

Thank you to my Lord and Savior Yashua, Jesus the Christ. Special thanks to my children, family, and friends.

To you the reader, may you be encouraged and uplifted from reading this book.

Shalom,

K. Lee

Table of Contents

Prelude	7
Introduction	11
Deborah	17
Job's Wife	25
Mary	33
Eve	41
Hannah	51
Herodias	59
Jochebed	65
Rebecca	71
Bathsheba	79
Jezebel	85
Naomi	93
Sarah	99
The Close	105
About the Author	115

Chapter Prelude

Elephants operate as a unit, entrusting each other to care for the other. They are only as strong as their pack; we are only as strong as the body of Christ. Every woman is needed today to help with children, both their own and those not born from them. Those with natural children are not left out because any woman can have a mothering spirit and help with children.

We are all children to Yah, but we are not all Children of God. None of us are grown in His sight. We are His children or not based on how we choose to live and what we accept. Would it not be our heart's desire to see all children enter the gates of heaven? If that is our heart, how can we not encourage each other and bring one another back to the pack and in alignment with God if we see the little children going astray?

The job of the female elephant is to guard the

Prelude

babies in the middle. There are a lot of women responsible, it may appear, for such few baby elephants. However, the threat can be great. We need each other to survive: the mother and the children, the man and the woman, the mother and the father. We all have a role in the cycle of life and humanity. There is not one part larger than another, no big I's and little You's.

If we have the mothering spirit, we desire to pour out what we have to others. But how many of us know that everything we may want to pour out is not always good? There are mothers who have been given the assignment of bringing children into this world. Who we can argue and say does or doesn't deserve to be a mother. This book does not argue that but points to the outcomes of children who have to survive in spite of it.

This book points to solutions we can bring to the world by harnessing and using the mothering spirit to help children who need it most. We are born with a mother because we need it. The Bible says, "No good thing will I keep from you (Psalm 84:11)." So yes, you need a mother. We never grow too old to have one or to get one if we didn't have one growing up. Some of us have mothers, but they may not exhibit the mothering spirit. They might fall short of what Yah intended for you to learn from your mother. This is the point of this book.

No one is perfect. We don't all have everything our children need, or even the children you may share a part in their lives. But if we can all unite and commit to raising children, like the elephant herds, we can better protect the children.

We cannot think of only our own children or assume because we don't have any, this assignment is for someone else. Not even for the reason that my children are grown, so I am done. You are a wealth to the family God wants to create, and He needs you, your gifts, and your purpose to help steer the children in the right direction they should go.

Prelude

Chapter 1: Introduction

When the Father created us male and female, He saw that it was good. I know there is much debate and confusion even for what a woman is in today's world. What used to be basic science, knowledge, and anatomy now is subject to opinion and mental toughness. You can think of yourself as male, female, or they.

SCAN THE QR TO

LISTEN TO "NO GRAY" BY JONATHAN MCREYNOLDS

There is room for gray space, but there is no gray in God. I love that song by Jonathan McReynolds, "No Gray," check it out when you can. He created them male and female (Genesis 1:27). It is ironic that I have to put a source for making this comment; even as I write this, I do a soft giggle.

Introduction

Not because I laugh at people who are in the throes of what their gender should be or how they feel about being born male or female, but because it points to the failure of not only women but men, too. I do have a book intended to be paired with this one, entitled A Fathering Spirit. There is a point to both of these books; the big picture is that women and men come together to make a family.

No matter how hard a person works alone or two of the same sex, they will not procreate without the help and mutual gift of what they both bring to humanity. There are no superior genders or people who are greater than the purpose of God. He brought us to the world so that we may populate the earth and take dominion (Genesis 1:28). He designed us male and female–but He chose to begin with man, Adam. A woman is a man with a womb because she came from Adam (Genesis 2:21-22). The Bible says the created will never be greater than the Creator; hence, women nor men are more significant and fit for worship than the other (Romans 1:25).

If we are not careful, we may grow to worship our gender differences. People can put women on a pedestal, and men can be done the same way. Women were created not to be worshipped nor to be compared to men. She was not created to be happy, and a man was forced to keep her that way. The concept, "A happy wife is a happy life," seems to point to one set of emotions and elevate them over another.

With sayings like this, is it a wonder why some may have a bone to pick with gender? However, the Bible says that Adam needed a helpmeet, so He created Eve

(Genesis 2:18). The Father said it was not good to have Adam be alone (Genesis 2:18). Having both genders is a good thing because we need each other to survive. As children, we need a mother and a father.

We need them both to be born, and we need them both to thrive and survive. Yes, many of us come from circumstances that are less than ideal. If we have an absent parent or come from a single-parent home, it would be easy to conclude we did not have both. Yet, the mothering and fathering spirit can be shown to you in many ways. God is a mother to the motherless, a father to the fatherless, and a friend to the friendless (Psalm 68:5-6, Isaiah 66:13, John 15:15).

So if your mother or father is near or far, suppose they died when you were young. If they never were active in your life or caused more pain than good, you can still experience what the Father offers to children of the light. You can find a father, a mother, and a friend in those sharing His spirit with humanity. A mothering and fathering spirit comes from God. A true friendship is a friend based on how the Word defines it. The world says it is your friend, but we find that it is not. People who have told us they would be our mother or father have also proven not to be.

We may say I am an adult, so having a mother or a father doesn't matter. But how many accounts have you heard of people selling their souls to the devil because they didn't have a father or a mother? How many people turned their minds, emotions, and will over to do evil because they were abandoned and felt that they had no mother or father? These people accepted the devil to

Introduction

be their parent because those with the power to mend broken situations are not doing their job of showing the light.

Yes, many are, but many more are not. It is the job of the Body of Christ for the men and women to strive to share the heart, the Word, and the commands of God with children. We are to raise up a child in the way they should go, so when they are older, they won't depart from what is true! Yes, they can turn and do another thing. We see that all the time. But they cannot deny that they did know what the truth was. They cannot say, they do not know what they do if they decide to go astray because they have a foundation in truth.

But for the many who never got this foundation. Maybe you didn't get this truth, which I will share over the next several chapters. I want to encourage you and say that you are loved. You have a mother and a role to perform for the children who need you. For those with adult children, you are not done yet. Titus talks about the older women leading the younger (Titus 2:3-5). Don't allow your age to rob you of your purpose. For the younger women, you were born for a time such as this (Esther 4:14).

Lastly, no matter your gender or how you identify, you were born for a time such as this. There is a calling on your life, and you are here on purpose, for a purpose, with a purpose. I believe this book can help the Children of God and those with a mothering spirit to have a resource to help them love God's children through the challenges, circumstances, and cares of this life. No matter where you are, what you had to do to cope, or how you had to survive, I want to help point to a sure foundation.

Introduction

Chapter 2
Deborah

I am unsure if you have heard of some of the things circulating about women who have ambition. These women are sure of themselves and their abilities. They are not attempting to compete with the masculinity of men, but they embrace the power of being a woman. A woman can do a job, and although she does it differently, it doesn't mean she shouldn't be seen as a good leader–or not a leader at all.

I know many countries don't see the value in a woman taking the lead culturally. Women are a helpmeet, and therefore, they feel she should stay in her place. That place just so happens to often be behind a man's dreams, purpose, and ambitions. This position is not out of protection but too often out of fear that her success would belittle the self-image he has of himself.

This relationship would appear off balance. It is not how the Father designed men and women. He de-

Deborah

signed the two of them to become one, which means you won't see where one ends and the other begins. Their gifts would, ideally, perfectly blend, and you can't separate the one from the other. But how often do you see the personality, dreams, ambitions, or plans of one completely drape over the other?

I would be the first to say I see problems in the feminist movement. Not because I do not believe women have something to bring to humanity. I believe in the roles God gave to women and men, and I also believe those roles were for their protection. We need each other, so I don't think women should demonize men, and likewise. I don't think men should belittle women and their efforts.

We will benefit best when we put our inferiorities aside to see what is best for the situation. In this situation, it was a time of war. How many of us have ever seen or been involved in war? If you have seen a war or heard about it, you might think of men gearing up to go into battle to fight for their country. You see their physical form, uniform, commitment, and bravery and may think–even for a moment, women don't belong here.

Women may be handy to mend the injured, but for her to have strategies and a plan for winning the war, it may be socially acceptable to assume a woman is not built that way. But do you know how many women have jumped into wars and never had to put on war clothes to fight? Do you know the women who made history because they were willing to use their skills to succeed in times of war? There is a right way to do anything and a wrong way.

Esther, with her beauty, was able to save her people alive. She was more than a pretty face, yes. Seeing her face initially captured the King's attention. Her personality and gentle spirit also made her a favorite. I am sure there were many other things that made her a top pick for the King and why he made her, a Hebrew woman, Queen over a foreign land.

In the Father's hand, your beauty can be far more than a physical attribute that makes a man happy. It can be a tool that He can use to help point man in the right direction. She approached the King and pleaded a case for her people, saving children, women, and men. She had a mothering spirit to care for those, even at the risk of her own life.

She wasn't the only one to risk her life in a high-stakes war. Deborah also stepped up for the challenge. During a war, the Hebrews sought God for what they should do. Deborah was a married woman and the first female judge mentioned in the Bible in Judges 4. She was the judge over the land, and I am sure it was no easy feat to take a leadership role in a society that didn't believe in giving women financial rights to their father's estates. They thought the man should inherit the wealth until three girls mentioned in the Bible broke up that theory.

The Old Testament is not as brutal as we may think. The Father can speak to any of His children at any point in history to get His message across. Whatever is for you will be for you, no matter the circumstances surrounding you. Deborah was a prophetess who gave a word to Barak, the leader of 10,000 men. He heard the

Deborah

SCAN THE QR TO

ORDER: WHAT'S FOR YOU IS FOR YOU! A PLAY BOOK FROM AUTHOR K LEE

Word of God, but he did not believe it wholly. He wanted Deborah to come with him to battle to have the confidence to fight.

Deborah, without hesitation, said she would go with him, but in her going, he would not have the glory of winning this battle but a woman (Judges 4:9). As they went up to fight the Canaanites, she told him, yet again, to go fight. He was looking at her on the battlefield, the same as the day prior. She repeated to him that he had the word of God on his side to win, but he felt it wasn't enough. He lacked the vision Deborah had. Her gift as a prophet was more important to him than her being a woman. He needed a helpmeet, and she was that for him. She wasn't his wife, but a helpmeet nonetheless.

As they went up behind the call of Deborah and directed by Barak, they pursued their oppressor. This kingdom had been oppressing them harshly for twenty years, so the fear of Barak could have been warranted. He wasn't certain if they would win and knew they would not if it weren't for God. There are a lot of false prophets, so he wanted, I am sure to be certain, she wasn't just talking but had the Hand of God behind her–not magic or good-sounding words.

When they overtook their enemies, the king took off running. He ran into the camp of another tribe that was friendly with Barak's people. She gave him something to drink as he asked, and he asked for her to hide him. As he laid down under a blanket to hide from Barak, she took a mallet and a peg. The woman took the life of the king, who fled. When Barak arrived to pursue the king, he found him already slain by the woman.

The word of the prophet was true! He had no glory for killing the king and winning the battle. The glory went to women! But the ultimate glory went to God! It shows He can use anyone to uphold His Word and doesn't ask societal norms for permission to follow through with His plan. He can use women to fight and defend from the middle. Women elephants are equipped to fight and protect if they must. We are powerful when we bear the spirit and power of God!

Don't feel robbed if you have had a strong woman bring you up. If you are a powerful woman gifted with leadership and the ability to war, don't think it dwindles your feminity. The Father can use both female and male prophets to win battles. He can use warriors of both genders to win for the Kingdom of God.

About Deborah

Deborah was the leader willing to do what the man Barak was scared to do without her help. She believed in the Word Yah gave about the battle and stood on it even when he didn't believe it. She went up against giants and won with the power of God.

Assignment: Don't get discouraged in well doing or feel overwhelmed when others lean on you more than they should. The glory will go to Yah, and He will honor you for your faithfulness.

Your Impact: Leadership Roles/Pastor: Women in this gift are called to leadership. You are bold, strong, and mighty in battle and belief. You are a help meet to those in battle and fighting challenges. Don't allow people to convince you that you are too strong or not feminine because you are in leadership. The Good Lord called you to the post of leadership. There is nothing too complicated for God, so you, too, can overcome. Lean on your uniqueness and position in God to accomplish any tasks you face.

Make it Personal

Reflection

Point 1: She heard a Word from God.
Point 2: She believed that Word.
Point 3: She encouraged others to move on the Word.
Point 4: She put her faith in action and Moved with the Word.
Point 5: She was quick to point to God as her Help!

Affirmation

I am strong, bold, and mighty with the strength I have from Yah Almighty in Heaven above.

Deborah

Chapter 3
Job's Wife

Deborah was a strong woman gifted to care for her people. The Father trusted her strong command and gave her natural and supernatural gifts. She was surely a triple threat. She could manage her own home, be an active judge, and be a prophetess all at the same time. So, she essentially had a family life, a job, and a ministry. How many of you have all three going at the same time?

It is not easy to strike that balance, is it? For some of us, this isn't your life, or perhaps you didn't have the support of a spouse. It can be hard, surely, to be a single parent and care for your house while also having a job and ministry that wants your time. It can feel like you are pouring out and not getting enough back in.

If you have to push people to do what God is telling them to do and then do some of the work yourself–leaving your job and family to do so is a challenge.

Job's Wife

I know it was not easy to go to war, be a judge, and work in the ministry for Deborah. Of course, there are many perks to being active in all three perspectives, but time is something you give a lot of.

Are you currently giving your time to build up others? Do you feel appreciated? If you don't have children yet or they are grown, do you feel you are pouring out a lot of your time and resources for other people? I feel and see that a lot of my time is spent building up others.

We are human; we all desire to be acknowledged for what we contribute. We don't expect to be worshipped, but we want our efforts not to go unnoticed. We want people to be grateful or have an attitude of gratitude. If we don't hear a please and thank you it can push buttons for us to feel some resentment or regret.

But the Good Lord above sees all you do for Him and others. He is the one that will acknowledge us and show us favor. If you struggle today to get the respect you deserve for what you do for others, be encouraged! When the Father notices you, He can send more obstacles your way or blessings. I know you might say, what do you mean send obstacles? You mean send me more opportunities, right?

Nope! When the Father notices you, He will certainly pour out His blessings on you. He will challenge you in ways that will make you more like Him. He will permit trouble to come so you can see your response and true heart. Sometimes, we think we are doing things to be nice, but we are doing them to be acknowledged.

It is alright to push the need to get your just-do, but be careful you are not doing things to receive the glory. We are to train children to say please and thank you and have a heart of gratitude. We are to let them know they should acknowledge people–and especially God—for all the good He does in our lives. Likewise, we are to thank Him for the rain.

It can be hard to thank the Father for His discipline if we only see Him as a giver. We must understand that He is a God that gives and takes away (Job 1:21). It can be hard to be burdened with loss when you do all you can to live right and treat others right. I know Job felt some kind of way when it seemed like his life imploded.

He was a virtuous man who honored God with all that he had. He respected God's command and taught his family to do the same. He was a landowner, and he had servants who worked for him. He was blessed and prosperous in what he sought to do. Life was good, and it would appear no cloud of circumstance was set in the sky to rain on his life.

Only it rains on the just and the unjust (Matthew 5:45). As he was living life, he was unaware of the conversation happening in heaven that would concern him. The Father and the devil had a conversation, and the devil said he was searching to and fro looking for someone who he could devour or tempt with evil (1 Peter 5:8).

It sounded like he was bored too, perhaps because he didn't find a challenge. Then Yah replied, "Have you considered my servant Job?" The devil said, "He serves You because he would be a fool not to (I am paraphras-

Job's Wife

ing, of course); if you take it all away, he will do what others do: curse you."

The Lord decided to entertain this theory for His glory. He owes us no explanation for why. So I don't try to present one, only to say this: He disagreed with the devil's accusation. He permitted the devil to do all he sought to do but not to kill Job. In one day, he lost thousands of sheep, camels, donkeys, and all ten of his children. He was heartbroken, and on top of that, boils were spread all over his body.

He was physically in pain and emotionally in pain. When he sought relief, he only found more pain. He went to his friends, and they blamed him. Accusing him of bringing this destruction on himself. I paraphrase and say, "They said, surely you did something wrong for this to occur to you. Who loses all of their animals and children and then gets struck with a disease unless they did something wrong?" But what they said was not the truth. He looked for relief in another place, the mother of his children.

She was in the best position to encourage her husband and turn his spirit. She could have said something wonderful, encouraging, and reminded him of God's goodness. Instead, she was not the wise woman who built her house but the foolish one who tears it down (Proverbs 14:1). She could have given Job the message of hope, but she used words of judgment.

Have you ever seen your spouse, a family member, or the father of your children struggling to provide for them? Maybe he is the reason they are sick or, Lord forbid, passed away. It can be hard to say anything positive to them, can't it? She was challenged to give life when she was in a dark place. She lost everything Job lost also. She was in pain, and in pain, she told him, "Do you still cling to your integrity [and your faith and trust in God, without blaming Him]? Curse God and die (Job 2:9)!"

She was rough, but as mothers, we can get mad at God when He takes away our children. Losing a child is hard, but losing all ten in one moment had to be crushing. She felt that God hated them because He took them and all they had in a moment. Blow after blow, her heart must have been stomped within her. The devil predicted that Job would act like this mother, his wife. He bet God that his servant would curse Him and die.

Yet, Job proved to be faithful and didn't curse God but began to curse himself. He started to curse the day he was born and ever being breastfed by his mother (Job 3:12). He, too, was struggling with loss and pain. As women, sisters, daughters, mothers, and grandmothers, we find it hard to accept losses we don't understand. We can blame God, or we can turn the blame to ourselves. Both of them were wrong.

When people die, it is no one's fault but God's timing. The ten children of Job were faithful to spend time together, give thanks to God, and gather more than most of us do now. In my family, we don't gather regularly in the same place, although we stay on our group chat often. We don't all spend time with God in the same way, and some of our lifestyles are contrary to God's commands.

Yet, we don't have the same things happen in our

Job's Wife

lives as Job did. He lost everything, and the Father told him, "Who are you to curse what I have blessed?" (Numbers 23:8). We can think to speak evil of ourselves to find the fault and place blame, but what if it has nothing to do with our mistakes but God's glory?

Job and his wife were restored and had more children than before. If you have lost children in the past, if you have been told you can't have them, or any other circumstance, take courage. The God ruling over life and death is in control. He has great plans no matter if you are here on earth or elsewhere. Trust His process even if you don't know, understand, or agree. He knows what is best for us all and is sovereign with all power to do His will. We are to remain blameless and keep trusting in Him, the One who gives and takes away.

About Job's Wife

She is guilty of tearing down her husband, the man called by God, when things were not favorable. When she experienced loss, she told him to curse Yah and die. She spoke out of her pain, and her pain brought her to think and say evil things. When we lose children, it can be hard to love and trust God. Hard not to try and find blame in others or God himself. Resist the urge and keep your faith alive no matter what.

Assignment: Watch Your Mouth. Stay focused on God's goodness no matter the test.

Your Impact: Peer Mentor/Volunteer. Encouraging other women who have lost children can help those who have also experienced loss. Encouraging children who have lost their parents or those who have sick children will give you a new wind and allow God to use you mightily. Lastly, you could encourage those who have had an abortion or lost their baby in an unfortunate circumstance. This is a loss for which many can feel guilt and blame themselves or others. They might want to blame their parents, their spouse, the father, or a father who blames the mother. Not only are the daughters of God impacted by abortion, but also His sons, the fathers. Be open to speaking to both if possible or recommending a man with a fathering spirit to talk to him.

Make it Personal

Reflection

Point 1: Life was good, and there appeared to be no clear reason for trouble.
Point 2: When trouble comes, there is not always a person to blame.
Point 3: How you respond to trouble, death, and loss does matter to God.
Point 4: Draw your strength, remembering how good God is even if you don't understand His choices.
Point 5: Know that this day, too, shall pass. Whatever you lost for God, He is able to repay!

Affirmation

I am loved, and the Good God Above knows how to provide for me and my family; I don't have to agree with His choices, but I will choose to trust Him.

Chapter 4
Mary

Can you imagine getting an incredible gift and assignment of becoming a mother to a child you did not "do the do" to create? I know it had to be hard for Mary to live the life she thought she was meant to live, to be excited about marriage, and for the things she dreamed about happening to be changed by God. The birth of the Messiah was a miracle, and this miracle also came with challenges.

In our lives, when the Father expands our home or heart through marriage, we don't always anticipate everything that comes along with the commitment. We are to love people and be committed to them for better or worse. It can be hard to stay with someone when the conditions seem beyond our limits. I know it was hard for Joseph to marry a woman who was already pregnant when he was betrothed to her.

He was looked at around town as the man who

Mary

couldn't wait and who violated Mary and their customs of waiting until after commitment to do the do. He, too, had to carry some of the shame of Mary because if the people believed he didn't touch her, then who's baby was she carrying? Why would he marry a woman who had already been touched? What kind of man was he to accept damaged goods?

In their time and space, this was a huge no-no. You had to be a virgin when you married, or you were not seen in the same way, especially if you were young and never married. Yes, those who have been married can marry again, but Mary was never married and already with child. It took an angel to talk to Joseph, so he didn't call off the wedding (Matthew 1:20-25).

This was a test for a marriage that had not started yet. How many of us feel that children are a deal breaker for you marrying someone? How many are hesitant to marry or date someone with children? It is not easy to involve yourself in someone's family and take their children as your own. It is a process for both to accept the new relationship. Be patient in this process.

Family members can sometimes be the worst judge when it comes to children. They can think you are not good enough because you don't have children of your own. They can compare you to a birth parent and all kinds of things that make us feel inadequate. Where the Spirit of God is, He will open a way for things to work out. Sometimes, communication is the issue; other times, it is about finding the problem and loving someone through their adjustment.

Joseph and Mary had to learn to love themselves as the baby formed in her belly; he didn't know her until after the birth of Christ (Matthew 1:25). I know of relationships that started when the woman was pregnant with another person's baby, the one dating her had to be okay with raising a child that wasn't theirs, and he was. He was there for the baby as if the baby was his. The two of them built a life together, and their blended family worked out just fine.

Don't think God has nothing for you because of your current condition. Or that because you have children already, you are doomed to be single or deal with men who don't want to help you parent. I am sure the thought also came across Mary's mind when she was uncertain on if Joseph would marry her or not. He was serious about leaving her quietly and moving on.

It can be crushing to hear someone doesn't want to be with you because you have children or they don't want to help parent the children you have. Be encouraged; the Father still has angels who work for Him and can bring a message to the right man who hears from Him!

I imagine raising Yashua, Jesus, was also not easy for Mary or Joseph. Joseph was not His Father, and He pointed to that truth all the time. It can be hard to hear, "You are not my" mother or father. He provided for the family, but Joseph was not in the position of His Father; he was a stepfather. He taught Him things, but His most influential teacher was God in Heaven. Mary also heard the Messiah tell her what He had to do because of His Father in Heaven.

Mary

Can you imagine being told things by a child for what they will or won't do? Have you noticed that His mom had to drag Him out of the temple when He was 13 and kept Him out until He started His ministry some twenty years later (Luke 2:21-40)? When Joseph and Mary were traveling, they lost Jesus and had to search for Him. Turned out He was in the temple teaching, and Mary had to be a mother to the Messiah.

It can be hard to impose rules when we have gifted children, but if the Messiah got them, we should all have them. Being gifted to teach, spell, and do athletics is a great thing. However, if working in your gift stops you from obeying your mother and father, you will need to pull back and operate in a way that honors them. One of the ten commands is to honor your father and mother so your days will be long (Exodus 20:12).

Yashua (Jesus) had to learn to honor both His Father and mother. We must all humble ourselves to the authority of our mother and father. This relationship, bond, and the definition of this relationship helps to cultivate our obedience to Yah in life. How you treat your parents does matter–even how we treat stepparents.

I also think of the women and families who become mothers and parents through insemination. Having children where you don't know the father can be tough. On the one hand, it is a blessing because a mother or family can have a child, but on the other hand, you lack the relationship with the father to know all you can about raising the child or children. It takes two people to make a baby, but it does take many more to raise them.

Make sure you have a nucleus of family support and those outside your family to help you adjust. Many moms can go through many emotions having children, especially during pregnancy. Having a partner who can be there with you in this process is priceless. I have had my mother, mother-in-law, sisters, and other family and friends. Don't underestimate the value of a village in helping you raise your child.

Also, there is no rule book for having children. We all need someone to help us, and Mary had her Aunt Elizabeth, who was also experiencing a miracle (Luke 1:39-45). She was the mother of John the Baptist (Luke 1:41). The two of them could talk about their experiences, and they gained strength from each other.

Don't be afraid to reach out to people and join a group to encourage you during your pregnancy. Your heart and attitude are important for you and the baby. A lot of science points to how you feel during pregnancy impacting the child. When you have the chance, read the Article by Talge NM, Neal C, Glover V. "Antenatal Maternal Stress and Long-Term Effects on Child Neurodevelopment: How and why?" (Access: https://pmc.ncbi.nlm.nih.gov/articles/PMC3710585/#R6).

So, we must be mindful of how we feel and treat our pregnancy. Everything you are going through matters and impacts your children. For me, I had to take time for myself. I had to learn to relax about how I felt about my body changing. I am sure Mary was taken aback by her body changing, although she didn't cause it.

Mary

Children change our figures and can impact how we see ourselves afterward. The body can stretch and leave marks after childbirth. Learn that you are still beautiful after childbirth. You are still loved and have a life after becoming a mother.

About Mary

Mary was a woman faithful to the assignment of Yah almighty. She was willing to believe and trust God even when that could lead to her embarrassment. She was entrusted to give birth to Christ and be the mother of our Savior. She was made to live a life that could have easily brought shame because of her culture's norms. She was willing to be whispered about amongst people and judged for what they believed about her, although it was not true. She lived with a stigma and gave all the glory to God, taking no glory for herself.

Assignment: To mother and spread the love of Christ, believing in miracles so that others can have hope and a future.

Your Impact: Church Mother. When you can exhibit the selfless love of Mary and point to the power of God, you can be used in this position. There are many who cover the shame of others. She was willing to take on the judgment, like many grandmothers who keep the children of their daughters. She is willing to mother a child she did not help to create but felt compelled to watch over and nurture. Women who don't have children can be used mightily in this way.

Make it Personal

Reflection

Point 1: Mary did not perform an action to become pregnant with this child.
Point 2: The baby was a miracle for her and for the world.
Point 3: She was entrusted to raise a child who she knew was special.
Point 4: She was called to train Him up in the right way with her husband, Joseph.
Point 5: We can ask God for anything, and He will hear His children no matter the hour or the season; He will make miracles happen for them.

Affirmation

Although the children I have may or may not be mine, they are Yours, and You will provide for them and me, helping us both to believe and lean on You for the things we need and desire.

Chapter 5: Eve

Mary was in a unique circumstance for sure, but there was another woman, Eve, who had a lot going on, too. She was in a situation where she was not born but formed by the Hand of God, made from the rib of Adam. She was not born with a mother and a guide to help train her. She was gifted to be the companion to Adam, the first man and father of humanity.

I am sure Eve was excited to be alive and to see all that was created under the sun. I am sure Adam took her around and showed her all the wonders of the land, sand, and sea. She was in a great position because the two of them could communicate with no obstructions. There was no devil to cause a division or separation.

The two of them didn't have to work to be healthy. Their bodies were naturally self-healing, so they had no cares or threats for life. They could eat from all kinds of trees in the garden and they were contended to enjoy

Eve

everything under the sun–until they weren't. They didn't eat meat, and the lion and the lamb could sit together. It was peace on earth!

We all want to return to this peace. We want to be safe as we walk around and enjoy the love of our lives. We want to build something with our spouse and see how God will create something new. In the Garden, Adam and Eve were chosen to kick-start humanity. The plans for bringing children here likely would have been achieved without pain.

That plan was changed when Eve did not follow God's command. Yah told Adam he had dominion over the earth and could go as he pleased. He was given authority over the animals and creatures on the land, sand, and sea. He shared this gift with Eve and told her of their privileges. He also told her of the only thing they could not do in the Garden: eat from the Tree of Knowledge of Good and Evil (Genesis 2:17).

Adam had no problem staying away from the tree. Maybe he was really busy or simply wanted to honor Yah. Eve, however, was curious about the tree. She didn't look at the tree with intentional plans to eat from it until tempted by the devil (Genesis 3:1-7). The devil told her that God was a liar, paraphrasing–what I do best. If you eat the fruit, you won't die, but you will be like God, knowing good and evil (4).

The truth is, she was already like God! The serpent doesn't look like God. He doesn't even look like an angel anymore. Yet, this creature thought to judge this woman and point to something she needed. It wasn't until that moment that she became interested in the fruit. Eve alone didn't want to eat the fruit. She thought of going and sharing this fruit with her husband, Adam.

She told him the same thing the devil told her, and together, they decided to side with the devil. Eve could have given the gift of life in her advice to stand with Adam, but she was part of humanity's downfall. Sometimes, we are in the position as mothers, women, sisters, and grandmothers to give advice that builds up, and we don't take that road. Instead of encouraging him to follow the rules, she encouraged him to break them.

Have you ever given advice that helped a person, male or female, do something contrary to what was in the best interest of God's will? Sometimes, it could be tempting our friends to date the wrong person, attend the wrong school, or pursue a career that can pay but does not fufill their destiny. We can push people to think what we are suggesting is good, and it could be, but what did God say?

The fruit on the tree didn't look rotten, it didn't sound bad and seemed reasonable. Eve and Adam made a fatal error of leaning on their own understanding (Proverbs 3:5-6). When they leaned on their perception of the fruit, that was what caused them to error. We don't know what we don't know. Many of us are perishing because we don't have knowledge (Hosea 4:6), and this is what the enemy uses to get us away from divine knowledge.

Not all wisdom is divine and will lead to a prosperous life. All things are permissible, but they are not

Eve

all profitable (1 Corinthians 10:23). The advice we share with others we want to be sure is in agreement with God's commands. He makes commandments so that we can be trained to become and behave like children of God. He says that my children follow my commandments (Proverbs 3:1-6).

The Ten Commandments are the ones we all want to know because God gave them to Moses so His people could please Him (Exodus 20). There are many more, but if we can start with these ten and the ultimate command by Jesus that says to love God with all your heart and love your neighbor as yourself (Matthew 22:36-40), we would be alright.

Adam and Eve are the parents of us all. They made mistakes that we all can learn from. Eve proved that we can make mistakes, and those mistakes have consequences, but they do not cancel out our place in humanity. She made the first sin of listening to the devil and then roped her husband into it. I am sure she was not happy about this afterward but felt guilty.

If you ever read the books for the Garden of Eden, you would learn that she tried many times to take her life, and the Father brought her back. We can think to kill ourselves, and I thank God that He can turn our hearts from pursuing it. If you feel like you have made an unchangeable and unsavable mistake, know that Eve was already guilty of that. She got herself kicked out of the Garden, but God still provided for them.

When God removed them and cursed them, they

were still given a way of escape. Mercy and grace were still able to show up and give them the strength to keep going. If you are feeling defeated by the decisions you made, be encouraged. You are still a child of Adam and Eve. He can still bless you and help you achieve in life. Your life is not over, and you are not trash because of your mistakes or poor decisions.

You are more than a conqueror with Christ living within you. He is here to help you live a better life and choose to be a Child of God, committed to living out the commandments of God with His help! The Savior is such great news because we don't have to be perfect.

Christ, the Messiah, was already that for us. We are joint heirs with Him, brothers and sisters with a Heavenly Father. We are born again under His blood and sacrafice and we share in the great work He has already done.

The mother of humanity birth sons and daughters. Two of her sons, Cain and Abel, have made biblical history when Cain killed Abel (Genesis 4:8). For some of us, we can relate to our children being dangerously jealous of each other. They can look at each other like enemies and not family. Being the black sheep can cause all kinds of emotions for children.

I am of the position that there would be no reason to justify one sibling killing another, but this is happening in our world. Cain felt inferior to Abel, and he wasn't willing to change his heart to please God and receive the same blessing as Abel did for his life. Some children will

Eve

not see the value in working for what they want to have. They may be more apt to take what they don't have or eliminate those who cause them to feel shame.

Killing Abel did not remove Cain's shame but caused him to bring more pain to himself. The pain of rejection or the spirit of jealousy helped him to push open the door of murder. But children don't murder only with their hands; they can also bully others. They can be oppressive with their words tormenting a younger sibling. They can push them into trash cans, belittle their importance, or make them feel unloved and unwanted.

If you see this behavior happening amongst your children, it would be good to put a stop to it. As a mother, we are to love our children and encourage their development individually and as a family. We want to encourage them to celebrate their differences but also their bond as family. We want to raise up our children in the ways of God so that they all can please Him and be blessed to live their lives.

Some children need reassurance, love, and someone to push them to do right. I am not sure if Cain had a track record for doing what he needed to and skimping on the things he thought were no big deal. Some of us are guilty of giving all we got to certain people and doing the bare minimum for others. We should not have this heart toward God. We should give Him our best and a first fruit offering He would approve of. He wanted an offering with no blemish or defects, and Cain wouldn't give that to Him (Genesis 4:2-5).

Give God the best of your time, talent, or whatever you have to show respect for all He has done for you and your children. The way we live impacts our children and those in our circle of family and friends.

About Eve

Eve was the first woman given the assignment of a wife. Her job was to build up her husband and be a help meet, but she became his stumbling block and the rock that impacted the ages. However, the Father was able to restore what was broken. He gave her children, but Cain became the first murderer because he was not willing to give his best to Yah. We have to do our best because our children will repeat our mistakes. We cannot control what is out of our control, but we can choose how we live and how we will respect God before and after a mistake.

Assignment: Be committed to extending and receiving forgiveness and be willing to allow God to rebuild the life you live with His mercy and grace. (You cannot live in reverse)

Your Impact: Mentorship. You would not be wrong if you feel like you need someone to help you navigate your life. We all need someone to speak to us and help us through life. It was not good for Adam to be alone, and it is not good for you to be alone, either. We all need someone to help us through. Reach out to someone and make sure you are not too critical on getting all the right answers. We all make mistakes, but having someone who loves you and is committed to helping you is far more valuable.

Make it Personal

Reflection

Point 1: Adam and Eve were placed in the Garden to grow together.
Point 2: Eve believed a lie that cost her what she had.
Point 3: She received mercy after the judgment of God.
Point 4: When she wanted to give up, Yah continued to pour out.
Point 5: The way we live does impact our children, but their choices define how they live.

Affirmation

My imperfections do not block God's plans for me, and despite my missteps, God can still redirect my faults to bless me and those I impact.

Eve

Chapter 6
Hannah

Eve might have failed in the Garden, but she dedicated her life to righting her wrongs and raising her children right. There are people in this life who exemplify the consistency that moves God. Their intentional nature to worship God in the good times and to call on Him in their times of need moves Him. But there is something that they do that pushes Him the most: their faith in His ability and promises (Hebrews 11:6).

Your faith is your confidence. However, what if what you have asked Him for is still months or years off? If what you asked Him for, you are not seeing. If daily you are being pressured and threatened to perform, but only you cannot or have not. In cultures where children are important and must be born to solidify or hold a marriage together, it can be hard to fight for a marriage based on matters outside one's control.

No woman can control whether she will have

Hannah

a male or female child. We don't write God's plans, but learn to trust Him. Out of our fear, we can be guilty of entangling ourselves with things that do not help our situation. I can understand why believers are tempted to speak to psychics about their future when their present becomes unbearable.

I do not, however, condone this desperate plea for help. I remember I went into a restaurant several times in Florida. There was a lady who appeared to be expected, but she spoke to me and said, "Wow, you are beautiful." I replied, "Thank you." She said, "Your future is so bright. You have an aurora around you. Do you want me to tell you about your future?"

She took me off guard, and I didn't know if I had misheard her. She obliged my puzzled look and replied, "I read cards, and I can tell you your future." Yup, I heard her correctly. She was a psychic who wanted to read cards to tell me about my future. I politely declined and told her, "Thank you, but no thanks. I don't need cards to know the future God has for me. I know it is good, so I am good."

She said, "But I can tell you more." I replied, "I don't need to know more." It was a hard time for me during this time. I was struggling financially, and I wasn't sure where things were going with my marriage. I was in a complicated marriage, had a little girl at this time, and it was hard to provide for her without a job. It was during a recession in the States (the US) after the housing boom went bust in 2009 or 2010.

Have you ever wanted something to change your

life so much that you could not rest without speaking about it? I love having a prayerful life because sometimes you just have to sit in the presence of God and sing, praise, and pray, then repeat in any order. When you are in need, people like that lady can come into your life to see if you will choose cards over the hope you have in Yah.

It was a hard time when I was praying not for answers but for my heart to understand where I was in life. The world was changing around me, and I was blessed to have a family and a place to live that was very nice, although the situation wasn't ideal. I knew it would get better, but I had to be patient and allow the will of God to work His way. I could not let my light afflictions rob me of my hope for what lies in the future for me (John 4:13-14)

Do you know that when I went to a different place to order food, I saw her again about a week or two later? She asked me the same thing, and I told her I remembered her from before. She asked if my decision had changed, and I told her, "No." My circumstances hadn't changed, but neither had my faith in Yah's will for my life. No matter what I was looking at around me, I still believed in the power of God. I then asked her if she wanted me to pray for her, and she replied, "No thanks," seemingly politely.

When you are dealing with a seemingly slow-changing process, it can be hard to keep working, to keep praying, and to keep believing when what you need may tarry. When you have to have a child to redeem your value, it can blur your belief in your self-worth and pur-

Hannah

pose. Hannah was a woman who prayed many times for a child and children from God (1 Samuel 1:10-11, 20).

She didn't change her heart toward God, nor did she grow bitter toward Him, but instead prayed more. She didn't allow her husband's love and affection to change her desire; he motivated her to pray all the more.

For some women, praying and waiting is the job. Children will come when God brings them, and He will have them bring no sorrow (Proverbs 10:22). God knows how to give good gifts (Matthew 7:11). Hannah prayed so hard one time that Eli thought she was drunk when she wailed, cried, and prayed, perhaps acting out of character for women in public (1 Samuel 1:10-17).

She didn't care what she looked like to others; she needed to hear from God. If you need to hear from God, don't be ashamed to pray publicly or privately. Go to the altar, pray at home on your knees, and seek the Face of Yah concerning your issue.

Having children can be taken for granted by those who don't know the stories of women waiting. The people who don't know the shame of women who have been shunned, mocked, made fun of, and threatened because they were not able to produce a male child specifically. We are not beyond these societal norms, and this norm is throughout the world, from the United States to The UK, from Africa to the Caribbean, Korea to China, from Christian homes to Muslim cultures, and the list could go on and on.

Many wives in history were divorced and killed

because of their inability to bear children or produce a son. Although times have changed, the viewpoint and societal norms for cultures have not changed by much. There are still pressures put on women and young wives to have children for all reasons under the sun. It can be a hard wait and a painful journey if you conceive and lose a child or children during this time.

Hannah didn't give up on praying about the children she pleaded for day and night. Her faithfulness to tarry in prayer and confront the Thrown of Grace boldly in faith moved God. She got what she prayed for and honored her promise to Him concerning her firstborn son, Samuel (1 Samuel 1:10-11, 20). When we vow a thing to God for something we ask of Him, it is important that we keep it (Ecclesiastes 5:5). Hannah kept her promise and brought her son to the temple for him to serve Yah in the capacity that He desired.

God is sovereign and in control. Trust His Almighty Hand to bring you a miracle concerning children. The Father has a plan for your children and you! I can imagine how good Hannah felt to be honored with her prayer answered. When we get something we have prayed for for a long time, the feeling of extreme power comes over us.

The Father is looking for our obedience (1 Samuel 15:22). It is in our seriousness to pursue Yah and His will that we may find the best present in life without the bells and whistles of Christmas. God answers prayers all the time and works miracles for His children. Stay encouraged that whatever is for you is for you. Things will not cancel out until the Father says it is finished. If He said

Hannah

yes, no one can say no.

If you have gotten a Word or a promise from God, heaven and earth will pass away before a Word from God will not come to pass. He is faithful from age to age. He does not back down or away from His promises. He will make them happen, and for the woman judged, shamed, and mocked about children, be encouraged. The Father can open and shut the womb (Genesis 30:22, 1 Samuel 1:6). We may not always understand why He does it, but I beg you to trust Him either way. She knew she needed a miracle, and the Father smiled upon her and showed her mercy.

About Hannah

Hannah was a woman ridiculed by a family member and her children. She was like the woman or wife going to parties who frequently got the questions or heard the statement, "No children yet?" We don't control when the Lord opens our womb or not. The right husband will love us regardless of that. Hannah's husband was good to her and loved her despite her inability to have children as quickly as his second wife. With the promises of God, though they tarry, believe, and wait for it, for it will surely come to pass.

Assignment: Use your gift of prayer and boldness to bring prayers before God to help build up children and families. Be consistent in prayer to the Father because the prayers of the Righteous avail much (James 5:16).

Your Impact: Prayer Warriors and Intercessors. The world needs people who are willing to pray. Those who will pray when what they believe for hasn't happened yet. To be bold in faith to believe that prayer works even if the results tarry. Hannah is needed in the body of Christ and certainly in the church.

Make it Personal

Reflection

Point 1: Hannah was ridiculed by family members.
Point 2: She was loved by her husband, and he supported her.
Point 3: She believed in the power of Yah even though what she prayed for took years.
Point 4: She remained bold in faith and consistent in prayer.
Point 5: She honored her promise to God when she received what she asked for.

Affirmation

I will be consistent in my prayer life to please Yah no matter my outcomes or situations.

Chapter 7
Herodias

Hannah was a woman who started with a closed womb. No one knows the reason why, and it doesn't matter. What is good is that she went to God for her promotion to become a mother. She didn't find fault or desire another life setup; she prayed for Yah to intervene right where she was. She kept a gentle heart toward Him, and He responded to her obedience and faith.

Not everyone has a virtuous heart to seek God to improve their situation. Some women will take this problem into their own hands. Sometimes, children are born outside of marriage or unions founded in love. Some relationships bear children out of controversy. I know it is tempting to shun the children born out of wedlock or to look down on mothers who became mothers too soon.

In the United States, back before the 90s, girls were put in alternative schools when they got pregnant

Herodias

during high school. Were they displaced so they couldn't serve as an example to other young girls? Were they put in a school to avoid the judgment of parents and students? Were they banished to another school because their shame needed to be hidden out of protection or to avoid embarrassment?

It is a mixed bag for sure on whether separating girls who become mothers young is a good or bad thing. Some people speak boldly about baby showers for babies who are being born out of less-than-ideal circumstances. I can understand the point of both perspectives, but no matter how you feel about the pregnancy, I think we should have the mind of Christ when it comes to children. Children are a gift from Yah, God above, and He even tells adults to be like little children (Matthew 18:3).

There is something that pulls at our imagination and hopes for the future when we are young. We can believe for anything and see the good in everyone. We can be honest about what we see and still have a heart to do good. When we are like children, it is no wonder how we can see the Kingdom of God. We have a heart closest to being void of an agenda. As we grow older, however, life has a way of making our innocent achievements merge into someone else's game.

Herodias, a woman in the Bible's New Testament, was married to a man, Philip, before she married Herod (Mark 6:17-29). There isn't much said about the marriage on whether it was healthy, toxic, or other. What we can see from the scriptures is that she wasn't satisfied with his achievements in life and perhaps wanted a man with more accomplishments. She left this man for his brother, who had a title, money, and prestige.

John the Baptist called her out on it and even told Herod. Although Herod didn't understand everything John said and its implications, he regarded John the Baptist as a good man (Mark 6:20). He protected him and wanted him to work his ministry. Herodias, however, hated his guts and sought every opportunity to shut him up–even by killing him (v 19).

Can you imagine this woman scheming so much that she would bring her husband and daughter in on oppressing and killing John? She had her daughter dance at a celebration for Herod. The girl did so well that he offered her anything in his kingdom. She could have gotten up to half of it from a dance (v 22)! The girl was unsure of what to ask for, so she asked her mother.

When I was younger, I used to think this girl was evil and plotting against John like her mother. However, after living longer and interacting with children, I have learned that not all of them agree with their parents, although they are obedient to them. I wrote a novel, Gray Space, about how the sins of the mother and father should not fall on their children, but their actions do impact them.

SCAN THE QR TO

ORDER: GRAY SPACE
A NOVEL FROM AUTHOR
K LEE

Herodias

The mother wasn't thinking in the best interest of her daughter but of herself. She was filled with anger, and she was willing to take from anyone to hurt the person she intended, and that extended to the people in the kingdom. John was a voice of hope to many and a great asset to the Kingdom of God. She allowed her selfishness to rob many people.

I know that no child would be pleased to have that rapport concerning their name of being the killer of John the Baptist. However, a mother scorn, who can contend with a woman who would stop at nothing to hurt somebody? So, the child might have felt they had to do what she said out of obligation. A lot of children growing up in a home where the mother is not of a pure heart can lead the children to do wrong. They may not get any glory out of it, but they must learn to hide their shame.

This woman was a homewrecker and messy, as my mom would call it. She tore up her family to pursue the brother of her husband. She was an opportunist and narcissist who involved her daughter in the scheme of murder. She thought to have escaped judgment, but the Truth remained. Those who have tried to commit one crime to cover another don't solve the core issue. Their own heart issue is ever present before them, and God will still judge them, even if they no longer hear His voice.

About Herodias

She was not a woman of virtue, so judging her and seeing no reason to love her or what she has brought into the world might be easy. If we are not careful, our judgment of someone can leak out into how we see their children. I know it can be tempting to say bitting words against fathers you don't like and people who judge your actions–or those of your mother. Don't allow their malice to become yours. If you are around children who need a loving embrace because they are weighed down with shame or guilt, choose to love them and not judge them.

Assignment: Don't blame yourself for how you got here, and don't blame the children of unlawful relationships and unions for the actions of their parents; have an open heart.

Your Impact: Welcome Ministry. To turn the light from being on yourself, it might be good to focus on others in a healthy way. Learning to embrace others and allowing them to welcome you can warm your heart and enable you to share the love of God that changes us. The way we used to be is behind us as we become "a new creature in Christ" (2 Corinthians 5:17). He can remove your past and help you envision a better future with Him. Greet the many sides of Yah and be a witness of His goodness to all those who enter the House of God!

Make it Personal

Reflection

Point 1: Herodias was never loyal.
Point 2: She was an opportunist seeking ways to get what she wanted no matter the cost.
Point 3: She would stop at nothing and regarded no one's life over her own selfish desires.
Point 4: She brought her husband and daughter into judgment for her murderous heart.
Point 5: She got what she wanted, the head of John the Baptist, but she did not erase the sin that was before God.

Affirmation

I will not allow my mother's choices and judgment to shape my heart to seek vengeance against those who have something bad to say because vengeance is the Lord's.

Chapter 8: Jochebed

Herodias was a questionable mother at best, but Jochebed's story is the complete opposite. She didn't abuse her child but was willing to give her life for him. A woman full of perfect trust in Yah's direction was Jochebed. She was the mother of Moses, another beloved of God. He was handpicked to bring the message and follow the command to confront Pharoah about the Hebrew people (Exodus 3:1-11). His assignment was the same: to go to the Pharoah and ask him to "let my people go."

No matter how many times he replied "no" and no matter the actions he resorted to, Moses could not waiver from his assignment from Yah. It is a great and powerful story, with movies and works to tell it. What I enjoyed reading the most about his life is how he came into being.

What do we know about the life of Moses? He was born at a time when it was dangerous for male

Jochebed

children in his culture. All male children under the age of two were ordered to be killed at birth by the Pharoah. Many children died under this law, yet many survived, and Moses is just one example of that.

If you haven't read the book of Jasher, it has more to say about Moses. For example, we know that his mother hid him for several months before she gave him to his sister to be set upon the river (Exodus 2:2). What made her defy a law to kill her son? The Bible says, "And the woman conceived and gave birth to a son; and when she saw that he was beautiful, she hid him for three months."

As mothers, we are to see something in our children that others may not. We can see the good in their timing even when other people say kill it. I remember when I got pregnant with my daughter Zoe. I told her father, and at first, he was happy. Then he spoke with his mother, and she told him that I should have an abortion and kill our baby girl.

Like Jochebed, I disagreed with his mother and was at odds with him because of his suggestion. Like her, I saw the good in a baby that wasn't here yet, and my mother told me to name her "life!" The name Zoe means life, and it was God's way of telling me that my daughter should live. Funny, we didn't look up the name until months later to know what it meant. When my mom first told me, she said God said that was her name.

When Moses was born, he was a wonderful child. He was pulled up by the Pharoah's daughter and brought to the palace. He went from a baby destined to die to being born to rise to second in command. As a child, when he sat on the Pharoah's lap at a banquet, he pulled down his crown. He put it on his own head (Jasher 70:2).

A wizard (magician), Balaam saw what happened. He cautioned the Pharoah to kill the child because he was prophesying of what was to come (Jasher 70:18). He thought that Moses was not acting as a child but as a reminder that his forefathers had taken Egypt before and he was here now to finish the deal.

The Pharoah, skeptical, was not convinced. Balaam encouraged him to kill the child regardless of the baby's true intentions, BUT God sent an angel to speak to them, appearing like one of the wise men (v 24). He introduced a test that would save the life of Moses. He said to place before the baby an onyx stone and a stone of fire. If he grabbed the onyx stone, he would die; if he grabbed the stone of fire, he would live (v 25-27).

This arrangement pleased the king, and what happened next humbled my thoughts. Verse 29 reads, "And they placed the boy before them, and the lad endeavored to stretch forth his hand to the onyx stone, but the angel of the Lord took his hand and placed it upon the coal, and the coal became extinguished in his hand, and he lifted it up and put it into his mouth, and burned part of his lips and part of his tongue, and he became heavy in mouth and tongue." Sometimes, to save our lives, we come out less than perfect–but this, too, is part of God's plan.

We might think of putting away children whom we feel lack a perfect condition in life, but I assure you that even their challenges can be used by God to ac-

Jochebed

complish His great work. Moses didn't want to be used because he stuttered (Exodus 4:10-14). When all along, God was the reason for it. It was to protect him so that he could serve Him later. If he had no stutter and grabbed the onyx stone instead, he would have been perfect for one thing: to die at the hands of Pharoah. In his imperfection, he could be used by the Almighty Yahweh.

About Jochebed

She was a mother who could see the beauty in her son long before anyone else knew of his flaws. She not only loved him but also believed in him and sought to protect him. She was honored by God and could breastfeed him and help raise him. She didn't lose her connection to him; he didn't lose his roots by living with the Pharoah and his family. It is not a bad thing to see your children adopted and raised elsewhere. The only sad crime here would have been her aborting his future and not allowing this beautiful baby to live.

> **Assignment**: Don't be quick to throw away a life because you can't see the beauty in them being here. Yes, you might not have all the tools, but somebody does, and most assuredly, God does.

Your Impact: Abortion. There are many reasons why women get abortions. We cannot allow the cares of this life to convince us that our baby doesn't belong here. We can see all the wrong happening or look at our lack and assume they would be better off dead than here with me. Look at how Jochebed responded. She chose to believe God to provide– even giving her a family to place her son. She was in his life, although she was not his main parent growing up. He grew to be a son she was proud of, and his family played a role in that. So, if you have a less-than-ideal situation, God can deal with that.

Reflection

Point 1: Her son was born at a time when laws spoke against him living.
Point 2: He was born without flaw.
Point 3: Of no mistake of his own, he adapted a stutter.
Point 4: He was not perfect, but God still used him.
Point 5: His mother was entrusted to still pour the love and fear of Yah into her son.

Affirmation

No matter my condition and imperfections, I can be used by Yah to accomplish His plans for my life and the Kingdom of God.

Chapter 9
Rebecca

Jochbed loved all of her children. She wanted them all to be used by God. Even when she should have taken the life of her son, she saved him alive for God's use. As mothers, we know it is not right to have favorites, but that doesn't keep some of us from making that grave error. With our children, what we cannot deny is that our children will interact with us differently. Some will love things the same as you, and others will be like mixing oil and water.

We cannot guarantee that we will have the same relationship with them all, and honestly, you won't. You have to love them all and see the value in each of them. It can be easy to love all your children when they are similar in behavior and actions. But what if you have what some could call a good and a bad seed? Can it be tempting to favor one over the other?

Rebecca, in the Bible, is a mother who has twin

Rebecca

boys. Before they were born, she was told she had two nations warring in her belly (Genesis 25:23). She was told that the younger son would rise over the older, and the older brother would serve the younger. She received a prophetic word that her younger son would rise above and rule the older son. Did she pick him as a favorite because of this prophecy?

Was she wanting to be on the winning side and clinging to him? Have you noticed that parents with a specially gifted child can treat one more favorably or spend more time with that child than the other(s)? Maybe they stand out not for something like gifts but because they are sick. It is nothing more sad than seeing children who love their parents feel rejected and unloved. Living in Jacob's shadow, I am sure Esau heard the news of the prophecy.

Is it possible his will to be bold, courageous, strong, and mighty in battle was to prove he was better than Jacob. There was no clear sign that Jacob was bigger than Esau; in fact, we are led to believe he was skinny. Yes, he was crafty and cunning. He was a great liar, so which child was clearly better than the other?

Maybe Esau sold his birthright for a bowl of beans because he never saw it as being his (Genesis 25:29-34)? He was also a wanted man for killing King Nimrod, as it was told in the book of Jasher 27:16. He saw himself as a dead man already. Instead of feeling the mercy of God to be alive, he grew discontent with that, too. Maybe this is also why God had a problem with Esau. He lacked gratitude and took that out on everybody.

I am sure he felt rejected, and he was angry. His father could have favored him because he wanted to cool his jets. He wanted to show the love of God despite his mother's rejection. Although she fed him, it is not clear how she showed him love. She wanted to love the child she chose. She even helped him con her husband into blessing him.

The sin of the mother wasn't Jacob's fault, but it did impact him and his mother. Stealing is wrong. Playing favorites is also wrong. We must learn to balance our love for our children and see them all having a purpose in God.

Esau got mad, I am sure, for having to serve his younger brother. Maybe he thought of killing King Nimord to get out of serving Jacob through death. Esau made reckless decisions, for sure. He didn't mind putting his life on the line to go hunting because he questioned what he had to live for and pursue–by his actions. We could see his brute force and willingness to fight anything as admirable and brave, but what if his anger played out for people to see? His dad tried to make him proud of what he could accomplish with his hands, but with the same hands, he took a life.

In Jasher 32, God instructed Jacob to go home and be with his parents. The only problem was that his brother was close; he knew that meant problems for him. They never got time to clear the air and talk through their issues before he left town after taking the birthright.

He prayed to the Father to watch over him because Esau sent a message that was not friendly about

Rebecca

him coming. When Esau thought of opposing his brother, he had to hide his hatred because the Angels of God were fighting his battle. The key to Jacob was not his ability or goodness but his ability to reverence the Father. He submitted to the prayers and Word of God concerning what he should do, and the Father rewarded him. He grew to become faithful, and he changed his ways and heart. This was the turning point for Jacob to grow and become Israel.

Not all children are perfect, and they all are flawed. They sometimes have to grow up into their promise and embrace what God has for them without bitterness, and He can make any side of the table you sit at great. If only Esau could have embraced his position, he would have seen the goodness of Yah, too. However, like Cain, he became sorely vexed to do harm and avenge his injustice instead of conceding and bowing down to the authority of Yah.

It would appear that Esau would have wanted to die before he served his younger brother. Time after time, when he thought of overcoming his brother and proving God to be a liar about the prophecy, he was proven wrong again. In Jasher 47:17-26 it outlines the agreement Jacob and Esau made after the death of their father, Isaac. Esau asked the son of Ishmael which portion he should take: the riches his dad had in Seir or the land of Cannan and Hebron.

He chose his dad's possessions, and Jacob took what was left of the land. This proved to be a mistake he would grow to regret. When the money was gone, and Jacob had inherited the land and was doing well, Esau wanted that. One concludes he was greedy, but I see a bigger finger pointing to discontentment that started from childhood. As adults, they were still like children in the sight of Yah.

Although Jacob grew older and realized the error of his ways, Esau only saw himself as a victim. He didn't take accountability but sought to punish the people who hurt him. Maybe he felt the most bitterness toward God and wouldn't allow Him to fix it. I pray that if you were born into a family dealing with squabbles about birthrights and the family's inheritance, you don't allow that to cloud your ability to act like Children of God.

About  Rebecca

Playing favorites and thinking to balance out the scales is not right. Rebecca had twin boys, and one son tended to be closer to her than the other. The parents picking sides led to the children doing the same. Their seeds are still fighting today. The parents could have been the ones who unified, but the mother helped to divide.

Assignment: If envy or jealousy is brewing in your heart against a sibling or another child of God, let it go and see how you can embrace what is yours.

Your Impact: Minister. When we struggle with something or have lived through it, it helps us love others through their transition. Jacob learned not to lie, steal, and cheat because the very same happened to him. He was humbled and didn't grow bitter; he grew closer to Yah. If you have experienced the neglect of not having a present mother in your life or one that showed favoritism of one child over others, allow the love of God to make its way into your heart. Forgive your mother, make amends with your siblings, and allow the love of God to heal all past afflictions. He knows the plans He has for you and everyone else, too!

Make it Personal

Reflection

Point 1: Rebecca was a mother of two strong sons.
Point 2: She could have been the glue to establish love, but she helped create the seed of jealousy in her son.
Point 3: The boys kept a long-term fight with one another.
Point 4: As parents, we don't control the prophecy but can control our response.
Point 5: Jacob learned the error of his ways and turned to God; Esau remained bitter and vengeful, missing the love of God time after time.

Affirmation

I will not allow bitterness and jealousy to rob me of the blessing that Yah has put on my life.

Rebecca

Chapter 10
Bathsheba

Rebecca had her twin boys out of love, but somehow, that love seemed to leak from her relationship with both boys. Trauma can make us feel like our decisions are valid. Maybe she thought Esau was a challenging child to raise, or he resented her because of her predisposition toward him. There is much we can ponder, but trauma should not be the driving force for how we live our lives.

If we allow trauma to take over, it can cause us to resort to adapting lifestyles, mindsets, and opinions that are contrary to the Word of God. Trauma is usually a side effect of injustice. The finger often is pointed at the victim, but it is not your fault. We can be minding our own business, and someone can predetermine to act dishonorably toward us.

Not everyone who acts horribly toward us is the devil. Some of them make evil actions. King David was a

Bathsheba

man after God's own heart (1 Samuel 13:14). He did honorable things to acknowledge the living son of King Saul, who was lame from being dropped. He could empathize with people hurting, but he, too, was the reason women hurt.

While walking on his roof outside, King David saw Bathsheba bathing in the water (2 Samuel 11:2). He lusted after her and sent his men to go and take her, as in kidnapping her (v 3). He knew she was married before he did all of this and didn't care. David wanted her and lusted after her. He raped Bathsheba, and then he tried to cover his mistakes when he found out she was pregnant.

He thought to cover his sin by sending for her husband, thinking he would sleep with his wife, and her being pregnant, no one would know of his sin. However, the husband was loyal to the cause and would not sleep or even visit his wife. He went back to the field where he was positioned by King David to be killed.

After her husband died, he was able to take her and make her his wife, but this wasn't what she wanted. This wasn't how the people saw it either; they still called her the Wife of Uriah. I know we can feel that people get away with the things they do to people. He not only kidnaped and raped Bathsheba, he also got her husband killed.

Anyone looking at this situation would grow bitter toward King David. They would ask, how can a holy God love a man who is so wicked? The Father has people of all walks who have committed all kinds of sins that He can redeem, but He also judges. King David did not make out like a fat cat; he was corrected for how he treated Bathsheba and her husband.

The child that she was holding was commissioned to die by God according to the punishment that King David set. Nathan asked him what he thought should be the punishment for stealing a man's wife and all that he had; he replied that he should die (2 Samuel 12:1-12). Some of us have fallen into the laps of men who have victimized us and assaulted us. Yah, never condones abuse and the assault of anybody, man, woman, or child.

If we think for a moment that God is pleased with this behavior, we are wrong. He will judge these actions, and although it may look like people get away with their acts, even the King of the Hebrews had to face judgment. All sins can be forgiven, but that doesn't mean our actions will have no consequence.

King David paid greatly for this horrible act. The only child the Father used from King David that amounted to something great was King Solomon, the child of Bathsheba. The Father said He would have a remnant, and although it was not His will for David to take a man's wife to bear a son the Father could use, He took this horrible situation and made something great.

No matter how children come into this world, if by rape, molestation, or violence that keeps a woman in a relationship she wants to leave. God can redeem the situation and give us beauty for ashes. He can clean a vessel, making it as white as snow. He knows how to deal with messy families, situations, deep trauma, pain, and anger. Be encouraged.

About Bathsheba

She was doing what was right but was targeted by a King and person of power who violated her. She was kidnapped, raped, and stolen from her husband. No matter who the person is, it is never okay to violate someone's God-given rights. The Father redeemed Bathsheba and gave her as a son King Solomon, but she lost things because of another person's lust. It was not easy, and I am sure she was grieved in one sense because the life she should have lived was stolen. God had to mend her heart so that she didn't resent the child that came from rape.

Assignment: Pray for the victims of abuse and their strength to not take out their pain on those who love them and the children who need them.

Your Impact: Counselor. Having a personal understanding of pain makes you a great candidate to help the Kingdom of God. When you have experienced trauma, bad situations, or circumstances and Yah pulls you out, you are the one He will choose to tell others of His goodness. The best pastors are those who have been delivered from much. Not all that you need freedom from is your fault. Sometimes, it is the sins of others that have planted seeds of anger deep within you. When the Father heals these areas and sets you free, you will see, like Paul, why you cannot stop serving Him and telling others of His power and goodness.

Reflection

Point 1: Bathsheba did not do anything to bring on the lust of King David.
Point 2: She was happy in her marriage and had no desire to pursue the king, a man of wealth.
Point 3: She did not resent her situation and inflicted pain on others.
Point 4: She allowed God to improve a bad situation by giving her a Son, which she was influential in raising so that he could be a man of principle.
Point 5: Her son did well for a long time, utilizing what could be argued to be the best parts of her character. He grew to be a great judge, full of mercy and balance, which I am sure his mom helped to cultivate in him.

Affirmation

I choose to forgive those who have abused me, and I will not allow hate to leak onto my children or create a barrier between God and me.

Bathsheba

Chapter 11
Jezebel

Bathsheba's redemption story is powerful, for sure. God can turn anything around that He wants. But what happens if He decides not to? What if He decides to write off your mothering skills and remove your children from having a long life?

We have all seen young children, teenagers, people in their twenties dying. Not all of them are dying dishonorably, but some are in gangs, witchcraft, drugs, and other works that do not give God glory–and can cause your life to be cut short. Being a mother is undoubtedly work, especially if your children are going down the wrong path.

I cannot imagine the pressure to mother a kingdom if you are a queen over a country. Ideally, this weight is shared with the king because being a queen carries a heavy load. She is responsible for a nation and will essentially mother a nation. Mothers come in all shapes

Jezebel

and sizes, ages, and experience levels. Some may feel you can be too young to be a queen, but how come?

Typically, a mother has two assignments in the constructs of God and family. She is first to be a wife after she has mastered self-control, and two, she will bear children in a family unit built with the structure of both parents. In our day and age, we know this process and family structure are not as common as they should be. Many of us live with one or no parents in the home.

They could be away at work, out of their lives, or something else. One thing for sure is that we all need a mother in our lives to help cultivate what women bring to the family. Women are to be helpmeets to their husbands (Genesis 2:18). They are to help the family bear heavy loads and responsibilities. She is not the head of the house but a great pillar of it.

What happens when the order is not arranged according to Yah's design? When life at home has a woman leading the show and the husband is playing second fiddle? I know this is not a popular subject for women to lead and men to follow, and ironically, vice versa. In our society, we want everyone to be for their own goals and purpose, even if they neglect the family. Many homes are filled with two people who don't want to sacrifice for the other, but yet again, they are both willing to sacrifice for what they each want.

This is not the dream team setup God created in the Garden. He wanted man and woman to work together in love and harmony. We changed that, of course. The order wasn't to oppress the woman or have the man dominate the woman. They are both made in God's image and in the spirit, we are neither male nor female (Galatians 3:28).

This doesn't mean women cannot lead and be leaders, but there is a role we play in the family. I know it is tempting to play the role we do in the world back in our families, but this can cause friction. Yes, no one is a superwoman, but we need to allow our husbands to become who they were born to be. We need to give good advice and sound wisdom so the family can be protected.

Jezebel was a wicked woman in the Bible. She worshiped Baal, and she had her son and husband do the same. We can not tiptoe around this subject. Witches are real, and women who practice dark magic and enchantments for power happen every day. These women are still women. Although they choose to be a beacon of darkness, they yield the power of influence by design as women and mothers.

Not everyone who operates in the design of Yah is an honorable vessel. He says He has vessels of honor and everyday use, or some translations say vessels of honor and dishonor. (2 Timothy 2:20-21). So yes, every mother won't be an honorable woman or even a woman focused on giving God glory with how she raises her children. Although it is not clear how many children she had, it is implied that Ahaziah was her son.

He was raised in the teaching of his parents, and he died two years shortly after being appointed king. The Bible tells us to raise our children in the way of God so that as they get older, they won't depart (Proverbs 22:6).

Jezebel

Jezebel was the prime force and power of influence over King Ahaz. She used her position as his helpmeet for her to rule the kingdom behind his title and command. She was pulling all the strings and coming up with all the schemes–likely with the help of demons.

She was such an influential witch in the kingdom of darkness that many churches talk about her spirit and how it disrupts churches and households today. She was a woman who would use her outward appearance to seduce men and then use her title as wife to the king to rule under the teachings of witchcraft–often full of manipulations. She was queen for using emotions, beauty, manipulations, and schemes to support her reason for killing, stealing, and destroying anything in her way to getting what she wanted.

She was a flawed woman and also a flawed mother. Children who were born in toxic environments have a lot to overcome, but with God, what is impossible with man is possible with Him (Luke 18:27). Her children learned her ways, and their ways were reinforced by the company they kept. Their lack of conviction and willingness to serve God rubbed off on their children and encouraged more devilish practices.

These unfruitful works might have produced ill-gotten gain, but they did not free their soles or grant them a happy life. Their son died young. The husband died a coward. Jezebel died by being pushed out the window by the two male eunuchs (castrated males) who often did her makeup. Her body was left on the ground, and the dogs came and cleaned up her splatter.

If we don't correct the wicked ways of children by their natural parents, their future will not be bright. It is hell, it is death, it is betrayal. When the Father does away with someone, He will ensure nothing else is left. No footprint of them will be left on earth. In the ESV Bible, Psalm 34:16 says, "The face of the Lord is against those who do evil, to cut off the memory of them from the earth."

Accounts like this are a warning not to live life forgetting to speak up when we see evil around us. We are to point out sin in hopes that we can correct through the power of the Word those who live contrary to their design and serve other gods. We were all designed to give glory to God. There is no one the Father can't redeem, but we pray that He draws you close (John 6:44).

About Jezebel

Jezebel was a beautiful woman who used her charm to manipulate men into getting what she wanted. She was willing to rob, cheat, and kill to achieve great marital wealth. She worshipped Baal, and she encouraged her husband, the king of the Hebrews, to do the same. Their patterns, beliefs, and practices were passed on to their son, who died two years after becoming king. Their parenting and disregard for Yah brought judgment to their house, cutting off their names from being great.

> **Assignment**: If you didn't have the mother you needed, become the mother others need.

Your Impact: Church Mother. I know we all have mothers we didn't pick, but one picked for us by Yah. We don't control this aspect of life, but we do control how we regard our mother and what we allow her to influence in our lives. Yes, we are to respect our mothers, but the Bible does not say we cannot disagree with them. Some mothers raise their children in dark arts, magic, witchcraft, and to worship other gods. Our job as women of faith, operating with a mothering spirit, is to train up the children who did not get the teachings we got. To share the Word of God to help those who are lost to become found. It takes patience to love someone engrained in wrong thinking to see the love and life in the Word of Christ.

Make it Personal

Reflection

Point 1: Jezebel was a beautiful woman who was familiar with adorning her face to be beautiful.
Point 2: She had a husband she knew how to manipulate, control, and influence.
Point 3: Jezebel was willing to lie, cheat, steal, and kill to get what she wanted.
Point 4: She taught these behaviors to her children and even encouraged them to worship other gods and practice dark arts.
Point 5: Jezebel was not granted a long life, and neither were her children or husband. Her body was erased from the ground, and she served as an example of what happens to people who are dishonorable to God.

Affirmation

I will not use my beauty to manipulate others, and I will be a beacon of light so that Yah may use me for an honorable purpose.

Jezebel

Chapter 12
Naomi

Jezebel was willing to use anyone to get what she wanted, including her husband and child. She raised her child to think and operate like her, which greatly cost him. Jezebel was not a mother one would want to invite into their families. She was like the dramatized mother-in-law everyone ran from.

If you have been married and heard the question, we are all asked when married, "How is your mother-in-law?" Many of us answer with mixed emotions. There are the wives who love their mothers and the many who feel judged by them. Those who feel no matter how much a woman does for their son, he deserves better than his wife. Arguably, they believe no one is good enough for them.

Can you relate? I had a mother-in-law like this who never thought I had what it took to love her son. She could have thought I was too old for him or that I was

Naomi

asking more of him than I should have. I am sure later on, she saw that I only wanted to help him. I couldn't save him, but my intention was to love him.

Sometimes, the grace on a husband is because of the wife. Are you an honorable wife called to serve a dishonorable husband? I know of a few, well if I am honest, I know of many women who faithfully served great men who were not the nicest to them. These are women who loved pastors to women who loved ex-drug dealers. There is a story in every woman that I hope one day can be told to encourage others.

There is no perfect story or one way to live life, and certainly not to marry. Naomi from the Bible is probably the mother-in-law we would all hope to have. She was a loyal woman with great values. She had a heart but was also logical. Her family came to Moab because there was a famine in the land.

Her family settled, and her husband died within a few years. Her two sons died also, all within ten years. She felt like God cursed her because of the events that befell her (Ruth 1:13). The daughters who grew to love her wept to leave her. They knew she was a wonderful woman who was not selfish but sought their best interest, even if that meant she was alone.

One of the daughters left crying to return to her former gods and life. The other, Ruth, stayed by her side. Ruth gave up her former life and culture to fully embrace Naomi as her mother. She wanted her God to become her God and to be joined to her forever (v 16).

Mothering Spirit

Some people you meet in life you don't have to bring into your world for them to attach themselves to you. Ruth loved Naomi like a genuine mother and was willing to follow her wherever she went. The obedience and commitment Ruth had to work for Naomi and their family must have pleased Yah.

While Ruth was working, Boaz saw her and took an interest in her. He started leaving food out for her and providing long before the two of them would marry. Ruth did not dump Naomi when the first thing smoking came her way, but she consulted her opinion about what she should do.

Ruth was not aware of the Hebrew culture but was committed to learning and following the advice of her mother, Naomi. Through her obedience, she not only obtained Boaz's interest but also won his heart. He pursued her and asked for permission to marry her. This woman, from a tribe rejected by God, loved her way into a family lineage that Yah prized. She became the mother of Obed, the grandmother of Jessie, and the great-grandmother of King David!

Talk about the tables turning around in Naomi's favor! It was a blessing for the Father's presence to rest on this family. You don't have to have a perfect outcome made with no struggle to be in the will of God. Mothering comes with death in the family; families break up, and people can hurt each other. Don't get angry about who leaves or stays. The Father "...will bless those who bless you, And will curse him who curses you; And in you, all the families of the earth shall be blessed (Genesis 12:3)."

Naomi

You don't have to come from a brilliant family to be used by God. You don't have to be a mother of living children to mother new children. Your children can be transitioned to heaven, and so can your husband, but when there is a mothering spirit within your heart, the Father can use you to bring life again. She told the girls what can I give you? I don't have sons. Even if I had new sons with a second husband, would you wait that long to marry again (v 13)?

Naomi didn't see God's full picture. He didn't need her body to give her children. Yah needed her willingness to be a mother to a woman who wanted to be like God. He used her to church the unchurched. She was the mother Ruth was not born to, but she needed to step into the role God had for her.

You might not be the natural mother for the many people God will send you to mother. You may have adult children, no children, etc. However, if God has called you to operate in a mothering spirit, you have everything you need to pour into those individuals. Don't lean on your own understanding and miss what He has for you and someone else.

If Ruth had turned around like Orpah, she would not have been the pillar we learn about today used in the Kingdom of God. The many people you will talk to will also be missing if you are unwilling to give what you have to mother someone else.

About  Naomi

Naomi was a woman with a bitter soul, hurt, and feeling low. In her low moment, she thought to pack it up, throw in the towel, and head home empty-handed. She had no husband, sons, or grandchildren. She thought she was alone. But God didn't see fit to let her return empty. He gave her a daughter who loved her. Ruth was a child who loved her back and would do anything to help take care of her.

Assignment: The Father makes no mistakes about who He brings into your life and when people transition out. Adopt the people He sends to you with open arms, accepting that they might not look like you or share your history. However, if they want to please God by staying with you, allow them to serve with you.

Your Impact: Adoption. Having the heart to adopt children is a huge undertaking. For the person adopting, don't be hurt if they have a place for their natural parents in their hearts—encourage it. To the adopted, the adoptive parent is not looking to replace a parent but to fill the gaps left by parents. When we hear of spiritual connections and people being connected by the spirit, they are not trying to replace God in people's lives but offer the mother or father spirit the person needs. Ruth had natural parents, but she also needed a spiritual mother.

Reflection

Point 1: Naomi was going through ten years of loss.
Point 2: She felt all alone and thought her life was over
Point 3: Naomi tried to send Ruth away, but she was determined to stay.
Point 4: The two worked together and cared for one another.
Point 5: Ruth restored to her what she thought she had lost, being a mother and grandmother.

Affirmation

I will allow God to use me to mother children that I did not birth and to use me when I think I have nothing else left to give.

Chapter 13
Sarah

Naomi didn't have the world to give anyone, but she gave out of what she had. She had a husband who died and two sons that quickly joined him. Naomi was alone with two daughters-in-law she had to provide for, which was not cheap. She thought she had nothing to give them–only she did. She thought she had nothing left, but God proved her wrong. She had a whole nation brewing in her. No, Naomi didn't have to give birth to Ruth physically to mother her into the next phase of her life. When she said she was done, she was too old, Yah said not so.

Another woman who thought her time to become a mother was over was Sarah. She was older than everyone around her—the age of a grandmother, not a mother. The thought of her having a child was laughable to her heart. Although she might have wanted to believe it, something held her back from fully embracing the concept.

Sarah

Sarah likely felt mixed emotions when she heard the news about becoming a mother in her old age.

> So Sarah laughed to herself [when she heard the LORD'S words], saying, "After I have become old, shall I have pleasure and delight, my lord (husband) being also old?" [1 Pet 3:6] And the LORD asked Abraham, "Why did Sarah laugh [to herself], saying, 'Shall I really give birth [to a child] when I am so old?' Is anything too difficult or too wonderful for the LORD? At the appointed time, when the season [for her delivery] comes, I will return to you, and Sarah will have a son." [Matt 19:26] Then Sarah denied it, saying, "I did not laugh" because she was afraid. And He (the LORD) said, "No, but you did laugh."
> Genesis 18:12-15 AMP

When we hear a word from Yah, just because we don't voice our thoughts doesn't mean He didn't hear our response. Sarah didn't utter a word, but she thought her response. How many of us would say the same thing if we were honest? Lord, I am old now. My husband is old, too. Now you want to give us children to enjoy?

I can see many of us looking at our birthing clocks, and for most of us, after our 40s, we aren't thinking of children at all. Sarah was way past that, so I can understand why she felt the way she did. Can you imagine thinking you were going to have a child all this time, to now be in your seventies and being told you will have a child? I am sure she had strong emotions behind her response.

God knows our hearts (Romans 8:27-29) and

the thoughts we think before we know them (Psalms 139:1-6). I am sure she was scared to be called out by God. Kind of like how we get nervous when our mother quotes words we said under our breath that she heard. It is like we are frozen still in an instant; our fear grips us that much, right? She was rightfully scared because Yah chooses to have mercy on who He likes (Romans 9:18). He can choose to be harsh or show mercy and empathize with you.

In the case of Sarah, He showed mercy. He didn't cancel His plans or judge her for her reaction. He used this time in her life to show her how big He was. Sometimes, we must be reminded that when we think all is lost, like Naomi, God can show up and change everything. How many "oops" babies are here today because Yah said they weren't finished yet?

I know I have said it, but I am good with children and don't plan on having any more. Yet, if I were to remarry again and the Father permitted us to have more children, I would rejoice about His goodness. I would eat all the words I said about not wanting to do diapers again and temporarily forget about the parts I do not care for because I am excited about the promise and power of God!

Sarah needed to remember God's goodness again. Have you ever wanted something so badly and it didn't come? She was growing old and thought she would never become a mother. Although she helped with mothering Ishmael, she still felt that there should have been more– and it was. This child was not the one He prophesied would come, but the actions of a desperate woman.

Sarah

Sarah desperately wanted children, so much so that she was willing to share her husband with a servant to have one. She grew tired of waiting on Yah and thought to do it herself. She thought any child would do, but this was not God's plan. When we get in His way, our actions can add a struggle that is beyond the scope of His intentions.

He knew the Word He gave to Sarah, but she needed to be reminded. When the Father loves you, He will remind you of what He said when you lose hope. I know it is hard to hold on when the Word seems to take such a long time. If He said you would be a mother, and you haven't had a child yet. If you were told many times that you would be a mother, but the babies kept dying. It is hard to be positive when there could be negative emotions surrounding pregnancy for you.

Stay encouraged, and know that God has a plan for you, and they don't cancel out because they appear to be complicated. He will push you ahead no matter what you might be facing now: old age, sickness, disease, doctors' words, family predictions, and so forth. Is anything too difficult or extraordinary for God to accomplish (Jeremiah 32:27)? I think not.

About  Sarah

Sarah dismissed a Word from God because she thought she was too old. She doubted what Yah said because she couldn't see it happening. But God did it anyway and made her a believer, humbling her and fulfilling His will to make her a mother. Though her time to have a child took some time, it did not cancel Yah's plans for her life. She became the mother to many nations through one son born of purpose!

Assignment: Don't think there is anything too difficult for God to do in your life.

Your Impact: Exhortation. Being able to sing and dance because of the goodness of God is a gift. To worship Him in song and expression comes from a deep set of emotions that bubbles over and must come out. If you have been waiting for a miracle to become a mother, your heart will be overjoyed when it happens. Sarah was filled with awe, and I am sure she had never second-guessed anything else Yah said in her heart or mind. When our faith is weak, we must be bold and ask God to increase our faith (Luke 17:5-10).

Reflection

Point 1: Sarah was old and thought she had missed the promise of becoming a mother.
Point 2: She doubted in her heart, and God heard her, although she spoke no words.
Point 3: Sarah was confronted about her responses, and she thought she would deny it, but God makes no mistakes, and He doesn't lie.
Point 4: She received mercy from God and not judgment.
Point 5: She became the mother of the Hebrew nation promised to Abraham.

Affirmation

I don't have to be perfect or young to be used by God; I am enough.

Chapter 14
The Close

There are powerful women, mothers, and families that have learned what a mothering spirit can do. As women with a mothering spirit, we have assignments and positions to fill on earth. We especially need to share love and instruction with all of God's children.

It is easy to think we have nothing to offer because we are not mothers yet–but you do! Hannah prayed for children and covered her children before they were born. We might think because we can't have children, we won't have them. Naomi mothered a child that wasn't hers. We cannot control how others will embrace us when we operate in the mothering spirit. Some people may seek to either embrace or reject us.

Rebecca played favorites, and I am sure she grew to realize that as she got older. Her son didn't appear to be too close to his parents as they grew older. He was

The Close : A Word to Mothers and Children

not concerned about them but about himself. He came to confront Jacob and deter him from coming, but why? Was he afraid he would lose out on the stuff his parents had? Was he protecting something he didn't know Jacob had no plans to fight him for?

Why would a son try to stop his brother from coming to see their parents? I am sure they missed him, and seeing him would do them both good. How can a child be so selfish to deny something his parents need because of his quarrel with his brother? But is this different from what children are doing?

Sometimes, there might be good reasons why we gravitate toward one child, but don't allow that to make you love the others less. Don't allow your healthy relationship with one to replace the one you could have with the others. If you have issues with your young or adult children, be like Hannah and tarry for them. Don't give the enemy your relationship and hope; believe God to turn it around.

We might think that there are more important things to life than family. I assure you, there is not. Although fancy houses are nice, they do not fill the hole in your heart. To be in a big empty house or a home with no love is lonely. To raise children who grow to dislike you or spend no time with you hurts. To have given your life to children and family who leave you and forget about you is like a knife to the heart. But all of this is part of life, and we quickly find a life outside of family is no life at all.

We all go to work and do our daily assignments to build family, hope, and a future. We don't have to build a family for ourselves per se; for many of us, we care about the Kingdom of God, all children on earth, and society. Where would any society be without children?

There are certainly times when being a mother is demanding. It can be challenging to raise children that are not yours, to try and mother a person who is hurt like Esau, to still believe in children when you are past your prime, to take the time to mother when you have settled into being a distant grandmother or a woman free of the burden of children. Yet, the Father can call your name and say, "Yes, I want you to mother."

Sarah thought she was too old to be a mother–she was more like a grandmother when she had Isaac. BUT GOD! He used her age to mistify the naysayers and got all the glory. Your miracle is a situation where God can be made strong. Don't lean on your own understanding and limit what Yah can do. Trust Him when He says He has plans for you.

When we are called to serve in the church, within our families, on our jobs, and wherever else He sends us to be mothers, we must show up. We have to have a heart for people, especially children. Not all children come nice and with great attitudes; some are broken, hurt, and angry. We have to be patient and allow ourselves not to be offended but patient in showing the love of Yah.

How much of a great thing have you done when you can help win a soul to Christ? Our job is to soul win. We are to help lost people, hurting people, and those who feel rejected to feel included and loved again. I want to encourage you that you do have an assignment—no mat-

The Close : A Word to Mothers and Children

ter your rage or if your children are young or old. There is plenty of work to do to share the mothering spirit Yah has given women who will serve Him by being His hands, feet, heart, mind, and eyes.

Your prayers can avail much! When we see injustice, we need to speak up about it and pray consistently for change. We need to believe our prayers matter because they do. We must know that even if we have made mistakes like Job's Wife, Herodias, Rebecca, Jezebel, and Sarah, the Father can turn it to our good!

He can make our shortcomings a life lesson to help other children succeed in life. Don't abort the plans God has for you. Believe that who you are and what you have to offer is enough in the Hands of God. He is here to listen to your heart. He wants to use you to be a blessing to Him and a benefactor of His goodness.

Hearing people say, "Good job, thank you, you have helped me," and so many other wonderful things from those who receive the mothering spirit we share is priceless. We must thank the Father for giving us the ability to love and share His love with others. The world needs women who think like elephants—who won't think of just themselves and their children but are mindful of all the children who need God on earth–adult children and youth alike.

We are to have hearts for those who are motherless, childless, and even husbandless. We are to help fill the gaps that exist in humanity, not by removing their mothers but by supporting her assignment. We are to train up children in the way that they should go. We are all like children to Yah, and our assignment is to help show humanity how to be a child of God.

Lastly, I must ask you: What's your assignment? What might be your job for the body of Christ and children who need you? What areas in life do you need help as a daughter or son of God? How can you use the help of a woman operating in the mothering spirit to help you? Adults need mothers, too, like Ruth. Don't think you are too old to have one or too old to become one. Is there really anything too hard for God?

If you have a living mother, be sure to connect with her and respect her. You don't have to agree with her or follow in her footsteps. We are told to honor our parents, not always because they are good, but because they brought us here on earth. We are to love them because learning to love them helps us love others. It is your first assignment, and how you treat your parents is also how your children will learn to treat you.

We are setting the example for how our children will learn to love and give love to others. If you didn't have this kind of relationship or if your mother was a toxic person, don't be discouraged. Don't think you get a pass from loving or being mindful of her. Don't think you will miss out on God's goodness, either. Sometimes, the mother you need now is not the mother you were born to. You can need more than your mother has to give, like Jochbed.

It is okay to hold the hand of women around you to help you get to the next level. Mary held Elizabeth's hand as she carried and became a mother to Christ. It is

The Close : A Word to Mothers and Children

okay if another woman may be closer to you at this moment than your natural mother. It is okay to embrace a step parent or mother-in-law to help you grow. For women to mentor you and for you to receive the love you need as a child of God. No good thing will God keep from you (Psalms 84:11).

If you are a mother who feels left behind by your children having other influences, try not to grow envious. We are to believe for the best outcome for our children. Sometimes, that includes them having other influences besides us. We might want our children to come to us for everything but don't be afraid if they need more. It's okay if you are not the prominent voice in their lives, and it becomes their spouse, mother-in-law, mentor, or pastor. Your place in their life is assured by God.

We are all meant to have a mother. If you are hurting because of the treatment or the absence of your mother, I want to invite you to pray with me for your life. It is important that the pain or anger you have toward your mother or your situation you release it. If you haven't forgiven her or feel that you can't, be open to allowing the Father to come into your heart to build a healthy relationship.

You two might not become best friends, and that is okay, but I pray the Father becomes the mother you need. That the mothering spirit can hover over your life and you not feel robbed. Allow His arms to wrap around you so you will not feel judgment, pain, or loneliness. I also have a prayer for the mothers. I would love for you to read both prayers.

"Father, you have been so good to me to use my mother and father to bring me here on earth. Thank you for the gift of life! Thank you for touching my heart. You are Good, Wonderful, and Wise Counselor. There is nothing you will have me to do that you won't help me through. There were times when I did not know your reason for things, and I still don't know all the pieces to the puzzle, but I trust you. I know you have plans for my life and my future.

I pray, Father, that you continue to show me how to love You and teach me to love and forgive my mother. My life with her hasn't been easy and maybe I am not easy, either. I want what You have for me, and I pray that You send me a mother with Your Spirit to help fill the gaps in my life.

Teach me what a mother is and the importance of her. Bring to me the mothers I need to grow in You. Show me how to love and share this love with other children that are mine and children that are Yours. Enlarge my heart to love my mother, children, friends, family, and even my enemy. Allow me to become more compassionate and learn what it means to empathize with those who need You.

Help me not to be so judgmental but to allow Your love to cover a multitude of hurt and pain in my life. Father, I give my relationship to You for my mother and me. I trust You will set me free from any malice, hatred, anger, resentment, or feelings of rejection I held in my heart– that I wasn't even aware of—so I can be free to love and receive love.

I thank You for hearing my prayer and being moved to change my heart and circumstances. Thank You, Father, for Your love and guidance. In the name of Your Son, Yashua, we say hallelujah, and so be it."

For the mothers, I wanted to pray a blessing over your life. Join me in this prayer.

"Father, we come to You with a unified prayer for mothers and children. We pray that You lift up Your daughters and women called to minister, love, support, and encourage Your children. We want to be a beacon of light and not emulate pain. We pray, Father, You search and equip us for our assignment. We thank You for not leaving us but being faithful to show us ourselves. Humble our hearts to realize our own shortcomings so that we can deal with them with Your help.

Bless us with the resources we need to mother. Bless us with food, shelter, solid emotions, stability in our relationship with You, and a heart to serve. Remind us of the simple things that move You. Help us not to be too busy pursuing things that we forget to mother and watch over our children. Help us to share what we have with other children who may need our influence in their lives. Help us not to become selfish or weary in well-doing.

We know, Father, You are bigger than our hurt, pain, and inadequacies. We want You to be the King of our lives and help us to know the right words to say. We want to be positive and think on good things. We want to help Your children by filling in gaps in their lives with Your love and Word. We need You, Father, to help us to have a word that will encourage and point people who need You back to You. May our actions and our words line up. May we become new creatures in You to be a testament to Your goodness.

Help us to be different and better than before. Show us how to love and receive love. Keep the children that are under our care. Help the children walk in their giftings and equip them with Your love and power. Father, rain down Your power to lift their lives and protect them through their life's circumstances. Keep them alive, hoping and believing in You even when their foundation is rocky. Give me the interest and patience to be Your hands, feet, mind, and heart to those who need You.

In Your Son's name, Yashua (Jesus), we say thank You, and so be it."

The Close : A Word to Mothers and Children

Chapter
About the Author

"God blesses those who work for peace, for they will be called the children of God." Matthew 5:9

Krystal Lee is proud to have authored this book and accompanying course to better readers' lives. She has a heart for helping people in their deepest times of need. She writes because she believes there is power in sharing stories and life accounts that others can benefit from and learn from. Sharing is caring, so she shares stories, ideas, and resources to better the lives of her readers.

In addition, Dr. Lee has authored over 35 books across twelve or more genres (adult, children, youth fiction, self-help, spiritual growth, novels, and more), in addition to ghostwriting and editing more than 20 published works. She has launched coaching programs and web courses that helped formulate many startup companies. Her specialty is aiding coaches, creatives,

About the Author

and service-based companies in defining their message, brand, unique selling point, and client avatar, as well as generating a sales cycle and structure for her clients.

Connect with ME QR

Empowering individuals is at the core of her work, and she is driven by her passion to continue writing. In addition to being an author, Krystal Lee is a business owner of multiple companies, a consultant, an ordained chaplain, and a speaker.

For more information about Dr. Krystal Lee, scan

the QR. To engage with the Coaching series and Monthly Meet up Group for Embrace Your Crown First Sundays at 4pm, please use the QR or visit InviteEyc.com and EmbraceYourCrown.com

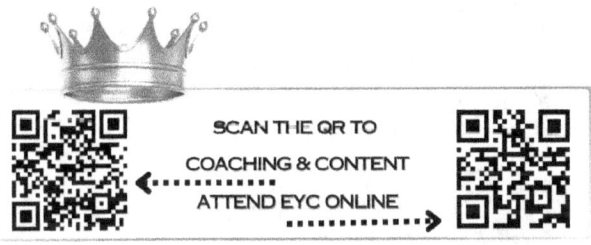

FREE GIFT

770-240-0089 EXT. 0
info@KrystalLeeEnterprises.com

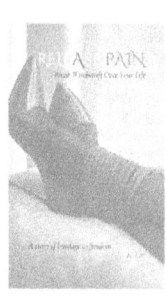

Shop Books from AuthorKLee.com

Explore over seven different book genres, and find something suitable for every member of the family.

Scan to Shop All Titles by K. Lee

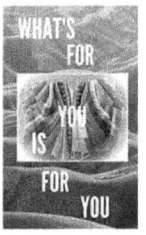

SCAN ME

Call or Text:
770-240-0089 Press Extension 1
Web: KLEpub.com
Email Services@klepub.com

It's time to start and finish   **YOUR Story!**

KLE Publishing specializes in helping people become authors. In as little as 15 to 90 days, we can help you develop your books and e-books and publish to 39,000 outlets! We also offer audiobook services.

Write, Edit, Format, Publish
We can help from
Start to Finish.

Explore and learn more about published authors affiliated with KLE.

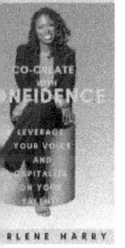

KLEPub.com

www.ingramcontent.com/pod-product-compliance
Lightning Source LLC
Chambersburg PA
CBHW070114080526
44586CB00013B/1293